E. Humperdinck's

HANSEL AND GRETEL

based on E. Humperdinck's opera after the story by the Brothers Grimm

illustrated by Yoshitaro Isaka
adapted by Eriko Kishida
translated by Ann Brannen

Fantasia Pictorial

Stories from Famous Music

Frederick Warne

Hansel and Gretel lived with their father and stepmother on the edge of a forest, for their father was a woodcutter.

One day, when they were so poor that there was only a loaf of bread and a little milk left in the house, their stepmother said, "Let us take the children into the woods tomorrow, and leave them there. For otherwise we shall *all* starve." And the poor father had to agree.

The children overheard this talk and when Gretel began to cry, Hansel said, "Don't cry, Gretel, for I have a plan." He then slipped outside and filled his pockets with pebbles.

Their stepmother woke them early next day. "Up you get! We are going to gather firewood. Here is a piece of bread each," she said.

As they walked through the forest, Hansel kept turning and dropping the pebbles. When they reached the heart of the woods, their stepmother said, "Stay here, until your father and I come back for you." And their father and stepmother disappeared farther into the woods.

All day long the children waited, but no one came. "Then they really have left us to die," said Gretel, as she began to cry.

"Don't cry, Gretel," said Hansel. "When the moon rises we'll find our way home."

When the moon appeared, the pebbles Hansel had dropped along the way shone white in the moonlight, and guided them home.

Their father was overjoyed to see them, but their stepmother was vexed. "Tomorrow, we'll take them even deeper into the woods," she said.

That night, the stepmother locked the door, so poor Hansel could not go out and gather stones.

Next morning they again set out early for the woods, and this time Hansel scattered crumbs of bread as he went. The parents led the children even further into the forest, and left them as before.

When the moon rose, Hansel looked for the crumbs he had dropped, but the birds had eaten every one.

The two children spent the night in the wood, and for two days wandered about, with only berries to eat.

About noon on the third day, a little bird, white as snow, landed in the tree above the children, and began to sing. When the bird took flight again, the children followed it by listening for its song.

Suddenly, as if out of nowhere, a beautiful little cottage appeared. When the children drew nearer, they could see that it was made of sweets and gingerbread, with a roof of chocolate, and windows of barley-sugar.

"Let's eat some," said Hansel. "I'll have a piece of roof," and he broke off a piece of chocolate tile, and began to eat it. "It tastes so good," he said.

"I'll have a piece of window," said Gretel, and she crunched a sweet barley-sugar pane.

Suddenly a voice said from the house, "Who's that nibbling at my house?"

"The wind, the wind, only the wind," the children called back.

The door opened, and an ugly old woman appeared. The children were so surprised that they nearly dropped what they were nibbling.

"Come in, dear children. There's nothing to be afraid of," said the old woman. She led them in and fed them on apples and pancakes and put them to sleep on a soft downy mattress.

"Are we in Heaven?" asked Gretel.

"We must be," answered Hansel.

The children slept soundly. They did not know that the old woman was a wicked witch, who enticed children in and then fattened them up and ate them.

"First, I'll cook and eat the boy," the witch chuckled to herself.

Next morning, she put Hansel in a cage. He could not escape, no matter how hard he tried. She made Gretel help her to feed him.

"When we've fattened your brother up, I'm going to roast him and eat him," the witch cackled. And all Gretel's tears were of no use.

Every day the old witch went to the cage to look at Hansel. "Put out your hand," she ordered, but clever Hansel put out a chicken bone instead, and the witch was too short-sighted to notice the difference.

"The boy won't fatten at all!" the witch exclaimed in disgust.

Finally, she lost patience. "Gretel, build up the fire for the oven! No matter how much we feed him, he isn't getting any fatter, so I'll eat him anyway."

Poor Gretel, while crying, had to obey, and soon there was a blazing fire and a hot oven.

The witch planned to push Gretel into the oven and eat her too; so she said, "Do you have a good fire going? Look inside and see."

"How do you know if it's burning well or not?" asked Gretel as innocently as she could.

"You little fool! Here, like this," the witch snarled as she stooped over and put her head into the open oven door.

Instantly, Gretel shoved with all her might, and pushed the witch right inside the oven.

"Ah!" shrieked the witch in a terrified voice.

And then all was quiet. The witch had burnt to a cinder.

"Hansel! Hansel!" shouted Gretel. "We're saved. The old witch is dead." And she ran for the witch's key, and let Hansel out of the cage.

The children hugged each other, and danced around the room. Now there was nothing more to fear. As they looked about the room, they found box after box full of precious stones.

"Just look!" said Hansel. "Let's take all we can," and he began to cram his pockets with jewels.

Gretel filled her apron pockets, and then said, "Now let's go home to Father."

They ran from the house, and through the wood, until they came to a stream.

"How do we get across?" said Hansel.

Then they saw a beautiful swan. "Oh, Swan," said Gretel, "will you take us across on your back?"

And the swan swam over to them. "Certainly I will," said the swan, "but you will have to go one at a time."

Then the swan took them both across, and they found themselves near their home.

Soon they could see the chimney of their house. The children ran in, and threw their arms around their father's neck. Their father and stepmother, who was sorry for what she had done, cried with joy.

Then the children showed their parents all the jewels they had brought home.

The woodcutter's family was poor no longer, and they all lived happily ever after together in the forest.